I hope
you enjoy
my
words as much
I enjoyed tu...
them into
poetry.

Father, May I

Collection I

[signature]

NARELL HUNT

Lilac Sky Publishing

ISBN – 978-1-7352351-1-0 (Paperback)

ISBN – 978-1-7352351-2-7 (E-book)

"Father, May I" is a poetic novel consisting of four chapters, titled by the inspiration behind the poems to follow. It dives deep into letters, and thoughts that have been inspired by experience and emotion.

Lilac Sky Publishing

4550 Jonesboro Road Suite A2 #322

Union City, GA 30291 United States

www.lilacskyllc.com

Dedication

To loved ones who have fallen too soon,
We miss and love everything about you.

Putting my thoughts into poetry,
The thoughts I consider deep.
The best way to express oneself,
Is to take these thoughts and put them on bookshelves.
Poems inspired by different thoughts that come to mind.
I welcome you to my words,
I welcome you to,
Father, May I.

-Narell

Table of Contents

PART I   1
No Tricks, No Magic … *Just God*   3
The American Dream   4
Grand Savior   5
Questions, Concerns   6
Forever Love   8
To Be Loved by You   9
Affirmations   10
Father, May I   11
The Protector   12

PART II   13
Sweet Serenity   15
Knowledge is Power   16
New York City Streets   17
Back in My Day   18
It is Calling   19
Recluse   20
Good Vibes make the Negative thoughts Subside   21
Fear Not   22
Whoosah   23
Cries of an Earth Angel   24
Countryside   25
Self-Awareness Leads to Growth   27
Let Nature Sing   28
I Can't Breathe   29
Not Perfect   31

PART III   **33**
Adjusting the Crown   35
Women Empowerment   36
Purpose   37
Parents are only Human   38
Nia   39
Deal Breakers   40
Happiness is Contagious   41
Virtuous   43
Look in the Mirror and Say, *"Hi, Me"*   **44**
Letter to the Veterans   46
I See You, King   48

PART IV   **51**
Barack & Michelle   53
When's the Right Time?   54
Why are you so quiet?   55
It's Rude to Stare, But …   56
Created to Mate   58
Grown Folks Play when the Children are Away   60
Anxious Attachments   61
Inspired by Pride   62
This Love of Mine   63

Part I

Letters to God

No Tricks, No Magic ... *Just God*

I travel in deep thought,
Thinking of you.
Hoping I'm making you proud,
With the things I do.

When life poses a problem,
You help me see it through my dreams.
I will continue to make changes,
Because Father, my God,

All I want is for you to be proud of me.

The American Dream

The more I work,
The less time I have to praise you.
I guess that's why they say you cannot serve thy father,
And chase money too.

Though I'm not trying to chase,
Just need to live,
Although you have proven to provide,
And that my friend,
Is no lie.

But it's not enough for all that meets the eye.

This world has turned wants into needs,
Material items I've come to seek,
Working day in and day out,
To live the life of luxury,
Or should I say,

"The American Dream."

Grand Savior

My grand savior,
The way you love me,
I sometimes feel I don't deserve,
Learning my lessons hard,
Some of my decisions,
I know you oppose.

But you stick by me anyway,
It's because of your love,
Today, I feel great.

It's because of you,
Today, I'm alive.
It's because of you dear Father,
I breathe the breath of life.

My grand savior,
Continue to mold me,
Help me do away with the things you don't like,
You are in control of everything Father,
Guard, direct, and protect my life.

Questions, Concerns

What is religion?
And does God want us to submit to one?
For a fact, he's in our hearts,
And when it comes to worship,
The Creator is the only One.

Allowing the Holy Spirit to guide us from within,
Guide us to preach His name wherever we go,
To speak of the teachings of His Son,
I was taught it was Him,
God chose for us to follow.

Some argue that there is no Jesus.
That He never did exist,
Could this be true?
Could His story be a myth?

Some say He was a prophet,
And that our modern-day prophet is the Honorable Elijah
Muhammed.
Others say that the priest is king,
Whichever way I walk,
I pray you remain on that path with me.

Because each of these walks leads to you...

Some of these systems that have been put in place,
Are doing the opposite,

Instead of righteousness,
Could it be bringing disgrace?

I want to always do what's right in your eyes,
Tongue only speaking with love and respect.
I work hard at doing these things,
Though I could think of a few times I have done the opposite...
Character conversant with human nature.

So, Father,
Which religion?
There are many denominations.

I am pleading for your pity,
Your daughter is lost.
But I will forever worship you, Father,
For it is you whom I trust.

Forever Love

Dear God,
I thank you,
For always being by my side,
Especially during such a time:
A time of trial,
A time of turbulence,
And times of giving up...

I ask that you remove the covers,
When there's no need to hide.
I thank you for protecting loved ones,
Keeping us alive.

Correct me greatly when I have wronged,
And shower me with your blessings,
Grace and mercy when I do what's right.
For without your light,
There is no shine.

I love you now,
And I will continue to,
Throughout the end of time.

To Be Loved by You

My Father,
The greatness you bring,
And your love makes me want to do nothing but sing.
Rejoice out loud,
From the changes you brought me from within.

I thank you,
For your mighty deed,
Is greater than sin.

Calm me of my anxieties,
My greatness,
Let it be shown,
Allow me to interact,
Using words that show you have put me on a throne.

With you,
I can never be alone.

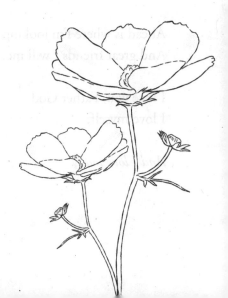

Affirmations

It's a great day,
It's a beautiful day.

I love the greatness you have in store Father…
I will think positive thoughts,
I will trust God with everything I do and say…

My actions and words will speak of a Godly woman's action and words,
Although everything I do and say,
May not always be considered that way,

But that's okay…

I will keep my head high,
I will keep my eyes bright,
My past is non-existent,
For that was last night.

Ahead is where I'm looking,
And great friends I will meet along the way,

I love you, Father God,
I love myself,

And I love today.

Father, May I

Dear God,
May I have a word?
I'm feeling a bit discouraged, broken down,
And Unheard.

Misunderstood even,
Being judged because of what people choose to see,
Making decisions about who I am,
Without getting to know me.

Father God, protect me,
Their assumptions cause them to act ill-hearted,
The evil they do and say,
Allow my spirit to ignore it,
Allow me to be strong,
Without being so guarded.

Allow me the strength and ambition to persevere,
For I am your daughter,
Keep me and my loved ones safe during our time of despair.

And during this time of disorder,
Father God, restore us.
We will follow your lead,
We will follow your order.

The Protector

My heart is positive,
So, I am.
My imagination is beyond me,
Because I am.

I'm a thinking thing,
Therefore, I am,
That last part was Descartes,
That's what he said.

God created us,
He wanted us to be great,
So, I know I am,
And make no mistake,
There's beauty in all that He creates,
He loves us now and He loved us way back then…

He gets us through it all,
His mercy has no end.
The Creator's existence,
I will always defend.

Part II

To:
Letters to Self
&
To My Readers

Sweet Serenity

Patience is a virtue,
At least that's what they say.
Patience is not easy,
We often learn this the hard way.

My hastiness can be like a small child,
Trying to grab a lit flame
As it dances about,
Beholding the sight,
Such a beautiful scene.

Only to realize we should've waited,
Before allowing temptation,
And lack of hesitation to make decisions.

Teaching myself to be patient,
Que Sera, Sera
What will be,
Shall be.

Take your time,
Relax your mind,
And enjoy your peace.

Knowledge is Power

Books are heaven,
And the words in them have power.
Digest what you take in,
And watch yourself go further.

Anything you want to learn about,
Just read.
A message from my grandfather,
An amazing man he was,
An amazing man he was indeed.

Knowledge I need,
One eyebrow raised to things that aren't helping me succeed...

Always be hungry for knowledge,
Always hunt the best feed.
Always know that you can obtain whatever information it is
that you seek.

New York City Streets

Thank you, Father God, for waking me up,
I thank you for all you have done.

Crown heights.
It's where it all began,
The first time I ever held a pen in my hand.

Corner store...
Location is stated in the name,
The men in front,
Serious about their dice game.

Ice cream truck,
Coming down the block,
Older kids opening the hydrant,
Because us younger ones were hot.
Prospect place was our block.

Shootings, crime...
That happens everywhere,
Losing friends too early,
First time I experienced despair.

Two dollars back then,
Can get you everything and everywhere.
Growing up in Brooklyn,
Free,
Without care.

Back in My Day

We did not grow up rich,
But just the same,
We grew up proud.
Vermin,
We had to get over it,
View them as past.

Wish they would go away,
And find another place to nest.
Thinking of different ways to get out of our mess.

We remember knowing that we must get our lives on track,
To escape the cycle of not being able to change our environment,
So, we can live beyond just being content.
We are all searching to live the life we desire from within,

To live our greatest gift given,

Life.

It is Calling

What happens to a spirit,
That goes unattended?
Not spoken to, heard, or considered.
When we make these great life decisions?

Does it stay quiet,
Like an abused child afraid to speak up?
Does it hide its emotions deep within us?
Could this be where our tears come from?

Consider your spirit to be a plant,
That must be nurtured and cared for,
So, it doesn't wither away, dry up...

Leaving you to be an empty vessel of what was,
And what is now no more.

Recluse

I see the good in everyone,
And that causes an issue,
Only seeing their good,
When their bad is far from minute.

I love with a pure heart,
And they're times when I've been shamed because of it,
So, I had to learn to create boundaries,
Make access to be limited.

The solitude's healthy for my growth and inner peace,
But am I losing touch with how to interact with society?

High possibility.

Good Vibes make the Negative thoughts Subside

My thoughts overtake me,
Leaving me to drown in sorrow,
Overthinking about everything,
Telling me to be better tomorrow.

Well, was I not fine today?
Was I a disappointment to my ancestors?
Did they want to turn over in their grave?

Just another crazy female,
Overtaken with emotion,
A cliché.

Fear Not

I dislike being frightened,
For there's no need to be,
Reciting advice I heard years ago,
Everything that is meant for you,
You will receive.

So be careful in what you put your energy into,
For it will surely come back to you.

Instead of waking up,
And being afraid of what the day may bring,
Embrace the day's journey with joy,
Take it in.

Smile when you want to scream,
And laugh when you want to cry,
Pick up that lowered head,
And hold it up high.

Do not be afraid,
For greatness is on your side.

Whoosah

Beauty in all things,
Even anger.
Use it like the plants use sunlight,
To help you grow.
Because if you don't,
Coming down from your rage,
You will find yourself regretting every word you spoke.

Cries of an Earth Angel

Not all days,
But some days I feel overly aggressive,
And today is one of those days,
The constant pulling and tugging of me,
Is causing me to become isolated.

Do not ask me for anything world,
Now, I cannot provide,
My cup is rather dry...
Leaving me unable to pour into you.
Once I refill my cup,
Then I will be able to.

As of right now,
I have nothing to give,
I must restore my soul,
Which must be catered to,
So, help me, help you...

By allowing me to restore my peace.

Countryside

Georgia my love,
Your home is enticing,
Full of nature,
Land and mountains.

Tubing down your rivers,
The singing of your birds,
Your food, your laughter...
If you were a woman,
You would be a work of art,
With bountiful curves.

If you were a man,
You'd be mysterious and dreamy,
A hit of you is like a hit of the finest herbs,
If you were a science,
I am your nerd.

If you are green,
Then I am your grass,
To me you are love,
And I came because I was sad.

Needing you to give me something I thought I could never have.

Where the trees have room to breathe,
And animals roam,

Where there's the distance between the homes,
Where laying on the grass feels like laying on memory foam.

Country life…

It's peace to the Earth.

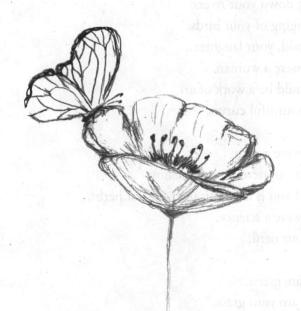

Self-Awareness Leads to Growth

Bad habits for me are attracting battles,
I can honestly say it's a flaw,
But I'm only attracted to these battles because I too,
Have unattended scars.

Once they heal,
I'll be able to see how far I've come,
Looking back on my life,
Surprised at all I've put up with,
And what I've come from.

Too nice, too mean…
It's hard to find that in between,
It truly isn't easy being a human being.
And you can't expect people to understand what you mean.

The only way to get through this is by living.

Let Nature Sing

You can never be lonely,
Your father is God,
And your mother is Earth.
Your roots are like trees
That sprouted from the Earth.

Your friends are the birds,
Who land near you to sing,
And the butterflies that land on you,
Sharing with you the beauty of their wings.

Yes,
As humans,
We require companions alike,
To love on,
Confide in…
Alone we were not meant to spend our lives.

Love yourself and all that surrounds you until that time.

I Can't Breathe

I had a bad dream,
Everyone in it was mean.

Men treated women,
And vice versa,
Young treated old,
And vice versa,
With such hostility,
Such animosity…

To witness tortured my soul,
Black men,
The oppression they suffered would cause any nation great stress,
One died,
Because insecurity mixed with hatred and rage wouldn't lift its leg.
You wouldn't believe how many times the man on the ground
begged.

This night was full of terrors,
The greed in someone's heart,
Allowed them to do murderous things,
Leaving their brethren to depart.

Oh, how I wish I had a voice loud enough,
For they would hear me say,
Don't allow the green-eyed monster to take you away,
To a place, you cannot escape,
A place where your conscience will not settle its rage.

For you never know who you will be someday,
So be careful with decisions that can negatively affect your
future in any way.
What a mistake I've made,
Silly of me to mix my dream,
With the harsh world of reality.

Not Perfect

I get lost in my emotions,
Thanks, Eve.
Though, I'm not upset with you,
Because to be upset with you,
I would also have to be upset with me.

Curious and disobedient,
Learning lies and thinking it's the truth,
What could this be?
Let's test the waters,
Not understanding that our choices today will impact our
future sons and daughters.

So much chaos,
So much death.
Might it be because we decided to put God to the test?
Break traditions and structures that were put in place,
All so we can live how we want,
Without limits,
To hell with restraint.

Now, look around and see if what we chose to be was right.
Instead of preaching life to be a joy, and full of peace,
We say to our children,
Be prepared for a fight,
Because life's a beast.

If we would've listened,
The way it is,
May not be.
Thanks, Eve.

But like I said,
I'm not mad at you,
For to me be mad at you,
I must also be mad at me.

Part III

To:
*Love,
Happiness,
Joy,
Parenthood,
Appreciation,
Laughter
&
Hope.*

Adjusting the Crown

Royalty...
The word best described when explaining the women, men too,
in my family.
But fellas,
Right now, it's not about you.

Pure breed Queens coming through,
High value.
On our worst days,
We are still good,
Tears turn from pain to breakthrough...

Breakthroughs leading to miracles...
In awe,
Of every single last one of you.

Women Empowerment

A woman's journey isn't the easiest.
The most underrated and the most underappreciated,
So, when a woman has it hard,
I get it.

Powerful,
Battling demons from within,
And we still find a way to love on our children,
And our men.

And with the undermine we face,
We still carry ourselves and our family towards victory,
The love of others is great,
But it doesn't dictate,
The glory God has set for thee.

With each mishap,
A step towards becoming greater,
One lap after the other,
Living life unapologetically free,
Until we reach the final floor of our elevator...

Our soul,
Living learning and growing throughout eternity.

Purpose

Letter to the Younger Generation...
I pray that life brings you great things,
And when these things come your way,
You welcome them in.

I pray that you understand that your dark times are temporary,
And that you bounce back,
From life's trials and tribulations
That will be on the attack.

May you always see what the world sees,
When taking a glimpse of you,
That greatness is yours,
Your dreams,
Be sure to see them through.

Grow into a being of a great mind,
Integrity and strength.
Allow only your light,
To shine from within.

Parents are only Human

As a parent,
Our children learn many lessons about life,
And when they mess up;
We sometimes assume it's because of something we weren't
doing right.

How do you make your child see their greatness?
For when I was younger,
I didn't see mine.

I felt like an outcast,
Only in school to pass the time.
Friends came and went,
Like Sam Smith,
I too became good with goodbyes.

I want to say the right things,
But have no clue on what they are,
I tell her she's wonderful,
And that her light shines brighter than the stars.

See outside of your issues today,
For tomorrow is coming,
Don't allow temporary feelings and burdens to get in your way.
The world needs you,
It needs you to stay.

Nia

God's glory,
His mercy magnifies,
Shining His light in ways many would not be able to justify.
An example is Him giving me you.

My dear daughter,
How beautiful you are,
Eyes that twinkle,
Brighter than the stars.

Your day is great,
Take God as your Creator,
Protrude power and grace.
Avoid the irrelevant negativity,
Avoid nonsense taking up your space.

In your mind, body, and soul,
Keep your Faith.

Your vibe is like the ocean,
Peaceful, serene,
But pushed to the limit,
Watch out for those waves to kick in.

Love to learn,
Develop a need to read,
Know that you are loved,
And know that you mean the world
To more than just me.

Deal Breakers

I need your attention,
I need your time,
If I can't get that from you,
Don't waste mine.

Deal breakers,
What you'll tolerate from what you won't…
Better have them,
Some try and take you off your course,

Better watch them.

Happiness is Contagious

That good,
Looks good on you.

You are rocking that positivity, *heavenly.*
Your grace,
That smile,
You make joy look so sexy.

I'm not trying to see your bad,
Those,
Past traumas that try and creep out when you're mad.
Consuming all that negativity will only tire us out,
Faster than jet lag.

Don't get me wrong,
When you speak your pain,
I'll listen.
It's important to speak it out when we're on life's mission.

Just know,
That when you're through,
That, that good looks good on you,
You are wearing that positivity,
The assertiveness in your voice can tame the wildest of the beast.

You're charming,
Mixed with the right type of confidence,
Words,
You do not mix,
Kind and stern,

Your touch, your embrace,
Day and night it's yearned.

Your love is the truth,
From here to Timbuktu,
Your self-love is announced,
No matter which room you walk through.

Your darkness,
We all have that side,
Secrets from me,
You don't need to hide.
In this bed,
We don't have any lies,
Each other's shoulders are where we lean when we need to cry.

When you walk you shine...
Created by the great divine,
Handcrafted in time.
Battles you've conquered,
Top of hills you've climbed.

So, when they see you,
They can't help but say,
That, that good looks good on you,
You are rocking that positivity.

I don't mind leaving my pieces unguarded,
Because I love how you check me.

Let's gather happiness and peace throughout this life,
And throughout eternity.

Virtuous

To women,
Who love to shine because they know they do…
Head high,
Walk tall,
Their presence can and will take over any room.

To the loving woman,
Who has nursed buried pain,
In you there is life,
You take away grief…
The antidote for strife …
Your household sleeps well at night.

To our soulmates we say,

Let us in,
For our love will be great.
Your heart dear kings,
Are ours to take.

To mine I say…

Molded just for me,
Our love will stand the test of time,
An example of what true love should be.

Love on me,
With every fiber of your soul,
Let God be our leader,
Until we grow old.

Look in the Mirror and Say, *"Hi, Me"*

Amid motherhood and chasing prosperity,
I forget to appreciate the woman before me,
Give thanks to the hands, for they heal.
A stroke of my finger down your spine,
Will quickly make you kneel.

I love my feet,
All it's helped me achieve.
I love my hair,
I do it up,
But I prefer it free.

Sound of my heartbeat...

My God gave me that,
Allow it to keep beating Father God,
I haven't fulfilled my purpose yet.

I love my laugh,
The way it echoes,
Especially when it comes from deep,
Within my soul.

I love my height,
Not tall, but almost short,
The ones that know me will truly get a kick out of that part.

I love my eyes,
The way they gaze when I'm in deep thought.

I love my past trauma,
It made me, *me*
Though getting through it,
Not always easy.

I love my aggression,
My need to be great.
I love my dominance,
But it's my creativity that truly takes the cake.

There's nothing about me that I would change,
Maybe just improve,
God will teach me,
For the divine is the only guardian allowed to take me to and
from school.

I love how I cry,
Every time I watch *"The Color Purple"*
"Dear God, I've always been a good girl."
You and I must never part,
Be my light always when I'm in the dark.

Pick me up high
When I'm feeling low.
I love me,
But I did not truly start,
Until it was self I started to get to know.

Letter to the Veterans

War...
What is it good for?

Freedom...

In our day to day,
We fight to be free,
Working our hands off to provide
Our families with the necessary necessities,
So, we can live how we want,
Come and go as we please...

But if not for you'll sacrifice,
These things would we be able to achieve?

I think not.

What an honor it is to write this to you:
All you've had to endure,
All you've been through...
Sacrificing yourselves,
So, your loved ones could be free.

I mean...
You've fought for people you've never met or seen.
That's why you cannot speak about military vets
Without mentioning humility, integrity, and bravery.

My grandad was an army vet,
Buried in the national cemetery.

His words cut sharp like a razor:
Type of man you can hide from now,
But he'll be sure to catch you later…
Style so wild,
Sergeant Hartman couldn't tame him.

Nat Turner was the first warrior
I learned about.
He was put to death on November 11, 1831,
Because he wanted what…?
   Freedom.
You see, it's not a Black or White thing;
It's an 'I don't want to be oppressed, thing,
I have arms and I want to fling them out in the sun, thing.
And I have a voice and I too shall sing', thing.

It's innate.
And we'll fight for it,
Even sacrifice ourselves for it.

I read in a book once…
"Is a hungry lion unfair or unjust?"

What you do for us,
Is the epitome of Love,

Thank you.

I See You, King

Black men,
Just how special you are,
Once was covered in oppression,
Masked with battle scars,
Some argue that you still are,

But look how far you've come...

The ones who have no problem with the words,
I love you...
My sophisticated brothers,
Can no one come before you,

My street dudes,
Understand that the streets don't love you,
Not the way you need to,
Be loved that is.

But if in that life you are embedded,
Use your wisdom for protection,
Teach the younger generations to learn from your lessons.

No matter who you are,
A woman has proclaimed her affection,
Your presence is majestic,

Take care of yourself so that you may live.

My hustlers,
Get your money...
And I don't mean negatively,
But I'm no stranger to term,
By any means necessary.

My family men,
The foundation you bring,
You keep the jails clear,
Your daughters walk the streets without fear.
Dislike that in our communities,
You are rare.

Being your sister makes my soul sing,
Oh, the value you'll bring.

Part IV

To:
Love,
Pleasure,
Romance,
&
Pain

Barack & Michelle

If you asked me to,
Love Patti Labelle,
For she said it so well,
It was something along the lines of,
In your arms forever.

Excited to win,
We're a royal flush,
No matter what hand is dealt,
We can't be touched...

This type of love.

When's the Right Time?

There's someone I want to get to know,
I think about him often,
The thought of him makes my skin glow,
I daydream,
Imagining his
love!

He takes me on trips with his lips,
His hands hold a firm grip,
Every inch of my body,
He has licked…

I'm only still imagining…

Bedroom, bathroom, and even the kitchen,
These lustful thoughts,
I wish I could forbid them.
How long should I keep my emotions hidden?

God, please lead.

Why are you so quiet?

Charismatically insane,
There's something about you that's not right,
But your conversation I like,
Because it's all over the place,

Like me.

Watching you is like watching my inner thoughts,
That jump around, but are in sync,
Just trying to find a way to be free.

I thank you for your company.

It's Rude to Stare, But ...

Locked in.

"You're just too good to be true,
Can't take my eyes off you."

Ms. Hill,
I know what you mean…
God went to work when creating this beautiful being.

So, forgive me if my eyes are glued,
A deer caught in headlights,
In aww of you.

Traditional with it,
What's your favorite food?
Clean clothes, warm beds,
'Come children, daddy's working,
Let's head to the living room.'

Modern-day with it,
Hot plate can't be every night,
I'm working non–stop for our future too.

Motherly with it,
What motivates you?
What stimulates that mind,
Keeps you intrigued?

You are a powerful being.
Who's better than you...?
Nobody.

Jackie O' with it,
"If I was married to the janitor,
He would be president."

Keyshia Cole with it,
Shouts out to all of you,
Whose partners are *heaven-sent.*

Created to Mate

My future husband, lover, and friend,
There's something I must tell you...
I can no longer hold it in.

There's another side to me,
I just can't explain,
I just know I love pleasure,
And as you can tell by these tattoos,
I don't mind a bit of pain.

You see babe,
I know you have the world on your shoulders,
Come and lay on your back.
Each stroke for each setback,
Each kiss takes away issues that haven't even occurred yet.

Let's intertwine our flesh,
Expressing our love with the passionate play,
Because it's never mere sex,
When we lay.

Every drop,
He was sure to taste,
This love is only for you,
Make no mistake.

Somewhat like a prison,
These walls will have you detained,
But in this holding cell,
You won't care about seeing daylight again.

Future husband, lover, and friend,
Show me that this type of intimacy still exists;
It's you who I'm waiting for,
Because only you can fulfill this.

Grown Folks Play when the Children are Away

Get on your knees.

Father forgive me for these words,
But I'm about to make him worship me.

That feeling is taking over,
And this tension only he ...
Can put at ease.

I stay calm, polite,
Keep my emotions wrapped up nice and neat,
But his words have planted seeds that have been growing,
And I'm about ready for him to start loving me.

Games,
I don't play them,
You got words to say,
Say them.

But right now,
I just need you to feast.

Look me in my eyes when you eat.

Holding me tight,
Loving me right,
Why are you still standing there...?
I said get on those *knees*!

Anxious Attachments

In love with love,
The thought of it excites me,
To love someone like never,
How enticing.

But it makes me insane at the same time,
You know the saying,
"If loving you is a crime...
Make me yours,
And I will make you mine."

Sing me songs,
Whisper sweet nothings...
Wrap me in your arms...
Let's share love,

'Til the end of time.

Inspired by Pride

Love,
Be vulnerable with me.
Let our imagination explore different 'Could Bes' and endless
possibilities.
Our hands, joined as we walk through,
High stepping through these galaxies.

Your laughter sets me free...

When it comes to love,
I was taught that the masculine leads.
So,
These feelings I keep,
Because you...
Won't be vulnerable with me.

This Love of Mine

I'm rarely lost for words,
And yet,
My tongue is tied.
I must love you for what you prove,
And not from what I fantasize…

This mind of mine.

It has created our future,
In this present moment,
You are mine;
Other options are null and void.

Heart captured,
From the first day we laid eyes…

I've come across others…
And the time we've spent notwithstanding,
But not even that could break how I've been hypnotized…

Writing songs to you,

This psalm of mine…

A woman should never express herself too soon,
But for you, I'm committing that crime…

Indeed, it is we,
For you my love is blind,
Call me crazy,
But I can't help,

This heart of mine.

Until Next Time...
Dance on one's hate for you,
Sing your heart out with glee,
Laugh out loud and continue living,
Focus on your loved ones,
And to the ones you love, loving.

-Narell